In a Split Second

MW01503264

Roberta Byram

IN A SPLIT SECOND

ROBERTA BYRAM

In a Split Second

In a Split Second

Mary Georgia Keppen

DEDICATION

This book is dedicated to my mother: Mary Georgia Keppen. September 29, 1930-April 16, 2014

She was an incredible writer and woman in her own right and she was proud of me; although I never knew that this was true.

Reading through her personal papers after she died, I discovered a woman who won awards, wrote poetry, kept a journal and did many things well that I was unaware of.

It was obvious, as well, that she was proud of all of her three daughters and kept every letter and news article or diploma that we sent to her.

I did not know.

In a Split Second

Roberta Byram

Mom,

I am very proud of you and acknowledge what an amazing woman you really were when you walked on this earth. I love you and I feel your presence with me often.

Love, Berta

In a Split Second

CONTENTS

In a Split Second

In a Split Second

WRITTEN BY ROBERTA GAIL BYRAM

PHOTOGRAPHS BY ROBERTA GAIL BYRAM

EDITED BY ASHLEY CULLEN

I share with you experiences from my life journals in order that you might be moved to stop and smell the roses right where you are in time and space. If you journal, find a day to read all that you have written so far and see where it takes you! There may be a message in your thoughts put to paper that will open your eyes and help you to see what might not have occurred to you! Our lives are full of possibilities waiting to be discovered. Yes, *waiting to be discovered,* as we hurry on through life filling every minute of every day with as much as we can. It may take a sudden, frightening event to snap us into the spiritual to see where we are really going and what we are really doing.

Roberta Gail Byram (http://bertsworks.com)

Pixels.com

FineArtAmerica.com

Edited by Ashley Cullen (Cleanup Artist Editorial Services)

In a Split Second

Acknowledgements:

Philip Newell, I thank you for presenting at Canyon Camp in Oklahoma at the Five Day Spiritual Academy. Your teaching on Celtic Spirituality helped me to claim my ancestral spirituality. I am forever grateful.

Jane, my artist friend who challenged me with books to read that challenged what I had been taught my whole life and to consider the possibilities of the created order.

Mary Knight, my best friend, who stuck with me even when I tried to push her away and for being with me through this life-changing experience.

Ashley, my step-daughter and her vocation of editing and words of suggestion and encouragement.

Tim, my husband who is patient with me as I live through all the life events with a passion and supports me through each and every one of them.

Daniel, who gave me permission to write about his story and share his drawings.

In a Split Second

Chapter One: Listen/Hear

Many aspects of one's life can change in a split second! One second I was driving down a street in a small town, and the next second, I thought I'd been shot. The sound was deafening, and somewhere in the far places of my brain I thought I heard someone scream a "blood-curdling" scream. It was a chilling, heart-sinking sound.

Being shot was quite a radical thought for me because I am never afraid in any areas of small towns, or even large cities when I drive through them. I simply wave and smile at all people. Everyone needs that. Almost all of them smile and wave back at me! Many have looked shocked like they should know me but can't place me.

So, for me to even register the thought that I had been shot was a mystery to me, and not for one second did I ever think it could happen to me.

In a Split Second

It all began when my mother died and our family went a little irrational like many families do in times of grief. My mother lived in Ohio in the area where I was born, and I live in North Carolina.

I invited my best friend Mary to go with me to take care of the final business and to be an objective bystander to help me remain stable, realistic, and unemotional in the midst of the final auction.

I needed to know that I was being true to myself and not unfair or ugly to any family members. In my grieving, I needed someone who knew me well enough to walk this path with me and keep me focused.

Mary was in the rental car with me as we drove past the hospital where my mother had spent some time and then through the neighborhood in this small town that would lead us out to the main road and then on to my mother's house.

It was in this small neighborhood that this incident took place, and one of the memories that will stay with me from this...experience...is the sound.

I will never forget the sound. I wasn't listening for it, but I did hear it. It was right at my ear and so deafening that it stunned me.

Immediately following the sound, I became aware that I felt no pain and wondered how this could be if I had been shot.

Then I remembered that the body goes into shock in times of crisis and often brings with it an absence of pain.

A faint echo of a blood-curdling scream hung on in my consciousness. It never registered within my being that the scream came from me.

At the same time, it occurred to me that I felt a faint whisper of air on my cheek, and I discovered within me that my driver's window pane had shattered.

I kept driving and did not stop for almost a mile past this incident that changed my life, but I did hear the sound that I was certain was a gunshot. I was not listening for it. I was not expecting it. But I did hear it.

Listen/Hear

What does it mean?

Silent, quiet-

Receiving babble?

What to listen for?

Is it hearing?

What am I listening for?

How long to wait?

Is listening shutting out?

Or being fully present?

Is listening awareness?

Birds conversing, wind whispering?

Crickets singing unendingly...

Roberta Byram

How to listen-absence of

Speech, noise, earth and sky-

Creation?

Why, what for, expectancy.

Do the rocks cry out?

Or does the sea roar?

Listen, listen

Come, hear, and receive

What then is listen/hear?

In a Split Second

I did hear the deafening sound like a gunshot at my left ear. That sound interrupted my life for quite some time. A week after this event that changed my life, Mary and I went to a restaurant to have lunch and took some of my grandchildren. There were 10 of us there, and so we needed a large table, and the buffet restaurant put us near the drink station.

We were sitting there eating and talking and laughing, and someone behind the screen where the drinks were, dropped the ice machine lid, and it made a loud noise. I know that it was not intentional, that dropped lid, but I responded as though it was my incident in the car repeating itself.

I dropped my fork, jumped in my seat, and looked at Mary. She was looking at me. We both responded when no one else noticed. A split second in time made us aware of that loud, abrupt noise when no one in that entire restaurant seemed to miss a beat in what they were talking about or eating.

No one but Mary was aware that my heart was racing, and I know that the blood drained from my face, and I looked like a deer in headlights. But no one noticed except Mary.

The next week, I was at the mall with one of my granddaughters, and I was holding her hand as we went up an escalator. A group of very loud young girls stepped on behind us, and one yelled something right behind my ear.

I looked at my granddaughter and said, "Those girls are very loud!" My granddaughter replied, "Grandma, I felt you jump and you squeezed my hand."
My granddaughter noticed that something had changed within me at the sound of a loud noise.

Again, I was visiting one of my daughters and playing cards with the children at the table. My daughter had fans placed strategically throughout the house because she did not have air conditioning, and it was summer. I was sitting in front of one of the fans because I am always warmer than everyone else!

We were talking and laughing, and the fan behind me fell over with a loud, unexpected bang! You guessed it. I was the only one who screamed and jumped out of my seat; I changed in a split second.

My response to loud, banging noises changed in a split second. I cannot hear a loud noise like that now without relating it to my experience in that car, at that time. It triggers fear, shock, and a sense of surrealism.

In a Split Second

Have you ever been somewhere or done something that did not seem real, but you were there, and you know that it happened? It is called surreal. It is almost as though the experience is an out-of-body experience.

The first time this happened to me was in a family situation where I had to deliver some bad news.

I did not want to; I was shaking; it was all I could do to open my mouth. People were going to be hurt. I was the one bringing the pain. Many people would suffer even though what I had to say was the truth and would have to happen.

I felt like my spirit left my physical body, and I could hear myself revealing the news. I almost felt like one of the recipients, only I could not feel anything at all. I wondered if I could have put an imaginary shield between my soul and my body because I would never knowingly hurt someone.

Whether imaginary or not, it was the only way I could get this information from my being. That was many, many years ago, and still I remember it clearly and acknowledge that it really did happen.

It was real. I was listening to what I was saying, but I did not really hear what I said in that moment. I just wanted it to be over and done with so I could begin healing.

My life was changed in that one split second. I was never the same again. From that point on, I could not be the bearer of bad news without fear, shock, and the feeling of being in crisis.

In a Split Second

One other time that I experienced this same phenomenon was in a canyon in Oklahoma. I lived in North Carolina and attended a week-long spiritual contemplative retreat each year.

The retreats that I attend are five-day spiritual academy retreats. There is a structured rhythm of the day to help those of us who are workaholics to get back to being balanced. Every day begins with chapel, music, and prayer.

After breakfast, we experience a presentation about the history or beginning of our faith, and it is more of an academic teaching. It is followed by one hour of silence while walking the facility, sitting in chairs on the property, sitting in the chapel, or just being alone in one's room.

This is an opportunity to not only listen to what has been presented, but also to hear what God might say to you. It is an opportunity to really hear something that you might not have heard before and to consider possibilities being offered.

It is a time to open your heart and mind to hear; not what the world says, but what God might say to you. Then after the silence, all come back together to an open discussion to share what is revealed to you. Discovery and sharing is an important part of the retreat.

In a Split Second

The day continues with lunch and free time and then back for another session and this one from the more spiritual side of things or the mystics or those who experience God in a way that might not be tangible, but more mysterious. The hour of silence and discussion follow, and much is experienced in that time from the heart to the "aha" in the mind.

Deep thinking and groaning of the spirit inside of you looks up at the wonder and awe of it all.

Then the retreat moves to chapel and Holy Communion before dinner. After dinner and a short break, we are divided up into covenant groups where we share all that we learned and felt (good or bad) in a small group to discuss deeply.

This is where we sort through the day and what we have discovered about our relationship with God and what God may have revealed to us.

The retreat days end with chapel and night prayer and then to our rooms. Five days of living the rhythm of balance, focus, learning, stretching, living in community with God and others.

One returns home from these retreats refreshed, joyful, joy-filled, balanced, and much wiser than one came to the retreat.

One always learns more about oneself through the Spirit of God speaking in many ways from the presentations, to the nature all around, to the close-knit community, to the overall experience.

It allows us to not only listen but to hear what God has been trying to say to us. It almost always changes us.

In a Split Second

One year, it was cancelled due to lack of participation. I was crushed because I looked forward to the week every year, and it filled my soul with the rhythm of the day— music, nature, learning, and a sense of community.

However, I obviously heard God speaking to me because I Googled this same retreat and looked for one anywhere in the United States.

Yes, there was one in Oklahoma! I called to see if my friend and I could still register, and the answer was yes! At that time, I did not know what God was calling me to do, but I knew that I had to go. Soon, my friend and I were on a plane flying to Oklahoma.

I wanted to go to this retreat, I needed to go, but I did not want to change; however, I did hear God calling me to go to the retreat even if it was in Oklahoma.

We arrived at the retreat in Oklahoma in the night and drove miles down into a canyon. It was so dark that we could not see very well in front of us. The road was a dirt road, narrow, curvy, and it went down, down, down. At the bottom of the canyon, we saw some buildings and a few people walking around.

In a Split Second

I wondered if this was going to be a nightmare, but we found someone who got us settled into the retreat center.

We would discover the next day that the retreat center was spread throughout the canyon.

As it turned out, this retreat experience in Oklahoma was surreal to me as well. Stacy and I still talk about it many years later, and we ask one another if it really did happen.

It changed my life. It took a while and did not happen all at once, you see, because it was too much to absorb at one time. Of course, I can look back now and see that it was life changing, but I didn't hear it when I was there.

Now I know that in the canyon, I discovered my "ancient calling" to Scotland, to stone and trees and nature. I discovered my connection to Celtic spirituality.

One of the books we studied was by Philip Newell, *Listening to the Heartbeat of God*. I was listening, but I did not hear it! Much later, I read in my notes that God is the very beat of life in our hearts, and I missed it!

Roberta Byram

I wrote…that when time is reduced to linear progress, it is emptied of presence! Philip Newell said that!

Of course we can listen, but if we decide there is no presence, how can we hear what we block out even if that presence is in our hearts?

I experienced nature, the teaching, and God, and yet I did not hear the message. I know that I was listening because I wrote about the experience shortly after I returned to North Carolina.

In a Split Second

Reflection in the Canyon

Why did God call me to the canyon?

The rocks...layered, solid, vulnerable,

Shapes, smooth, sharp, imagination.

Orange, rust, gray, mossy green.

The rocks silently calling to me

To be one with creation.

The trees...vibrant, orange, red, yellow-

Glowing, shouting out God's glory-

Pine, fir, deep green, leaning, depth.

Dying tree, huge, black, strong

Against backdrop of vibrancy.

Huge black branches stretching to heaven

Begging to drop to its knees.

Making a statement of boldness, strength, audacity to stand so...

Roberta Byram

The sound...bleating wild mountain goats,

Glimpsed rarely...

The crows cawing each to the other

All birds singing God's praise--

Attention all the earth!

To the glory of God all around!

The smells...of crisp air and earth,

Damp leaves, mist, standing water

Freshness of new day.

The touch...of God,

In blowing leaves swirling about me,

Droplets inviting me to look up.

The healing rays of sunlight

Warming my face, body.

In a Split Second

Calling, calling in and through the canyon.

The doe who daringly stepped in front of me

Beautiful, unafraid, boldly, silently

Questioning me—eye to eye.

Silent conversation—

Knowing, connecting, oneness for a moment—

Or two or three.

Human, animal: one with nature.

Turning, white tail, large, brilliant;

Pointing me upward

As she returned to where she came from.

Magnificent, majestic, rock, sky,

Trees, earth, goats and deer.

Why did God bring me to the canyon?

In a Split Second

As I read this several years later, I remember I wanted to cry. Where was the girly girl afraid of insects and snakes? I do not remember being afraid in the canyon (rattlesnakes reside there!). I seemed to be completely at one with God and nature.

When my North Carolina retreat was cancelled, I experienced fear, shock, and a crisis in my life and responded in a way that changed my life.

The week-long retreat in Oklahoma held those same emotions because I knew who I was when I arrived, and I did not want to hear anything else.

I closed myself off and put myself in a box, tied a pretty ribbon on the box and did not want to hear anything that was going to change my life.

This retreat was supposed to be my break, a rest, a chance to learn, worship, and enjoy the silence. I was not ready for this to be a life-changing experience, and so I was determined to listen and participate, but I did not want to hear.

It was a surreal experience. My delivery of bad news to my family was surreal. This canyon retreat was surreal. The sound of a gunshot in Ohio was surreal.

As I look back and ask myself if these experiences really did happen—now it feels like I was taken out of time and plopped down somewhere that was not real, but just surreal.

The only problem is...I know that they were real...just like my split second in the car was real and got my attention.

Listening and hearing are not the same thing. When we hear something, we take it into our very being but when we just listen...as the saying goes...it can go into one ear and out the other.

We do not realize that any experience in our lives can change our lives over a period of years or in a split second.

In a Split Second

Chapter Two: Mystery

Hear Ye!

God created all.

Rocks, trees, canyon.

God created all.

You and me and humanity.

Do we listen; do we hear?

The Creator bringing us together.

Is the image of God

Familiar or alien?

Hidden beneath the layers

Of all we pile on in our lives

How can we hear; how can we see?

Is the Creator and creation known?

In a Split Second

The image of God is birthed

Into our world of humanness

Revelation, self-giving, love

Jesus Incarnate!

Visible yet invisible

Seen and unseen

Understood, yet misunderstood

Jesus, come to life.

Layers of choice, baggage

Complacency, piled so high

That recognition is

Barely visible.

Paralyzed with fear,

Pride, all the others

Unable to see clearly

Jesus Incarnate.

The one who was

And is and is to come.

The incarnate Imago Dei

Can we hear; can we see?

Wooing us.

Calling us to

Imago Dei within us.

To connect, to embrace,

To love.

To "be"

To recognize each other

To know each

One as one.

In a Split Second

So distracted we are

By free will and choice

And baggage; getting our attention

Is monumental!

Love startles us

With recognition through

A relationship stronger than

All the others.

Jesus reveals

The depth, height, breadth, width

Of love for us as we are startled

With his incarnation.

Breaking into history.

Roberta Byram

LISTEN! Turning our free will, our choices

Upside down—all around

HEAR YE! Pay attention!

Calling us to attention

To who we really are—to recognize the

Image of God's likeness inside

Of our soul that God created.

Crucify him!

But He is God! Come to Earth—crucify him!

Look and see—the image of God incarnate, do we—

Recognize, hear, and see?

At what length

Did he stretch to call us back to him?

In a Split Second

To come out of hiding, to reclaim.

Who we are?

Do we listen, hear, and see

God's creation all around

You and me and trees and rocks

Shouting! Hear ye! Hear ye!

Hear what? Can we hear mystery? Was I shot? What to listen for now? Was it my turn to be a child again and in the arms of God?

Obviously, it was not my time to be a child again and swung round and round in the arms of God or taken to the other side because I became aware of a soft, calm voice repeating over and over, "pull over—pull over— pull over."

That could not be my best friend, Mary, who is boisterous, loud, and all over the place (just like I am!). "Pull over—pull over—pull over."

The gentleness of her voice wrapped around me, and instead of looking to my birthing image, I tried to focus on the softness of her voice persuading me to do something...like pull the car over and stop driving. All of these things were taking place in my mind in just seconds...happening in split seconds. No time to think about anything...just react.

The mystery is how on earth did I drive a mile with my eyes opened or closed? Does shock allow you to focus, to react, or to function? Since that time, I have wondered if angels were present and steering my car to safety.

In a Split Second

I even drove over a bridge that was over another road below. It is a mystery to me that we did not just go over the side of the bridge. It is a mystery to me that my friend Mary was so calm and gentle and simply guided me in a way that was the only way I could be reached. This situation...all of it was a mystery indeed.

A split second and I stopped the car as I became aware of Mary's soothing voice saying...pull over.

Many aspects of one's life can change in a split second! Just after I thought I'd been shot, I remember looking for my angels and waiting for them to take me to Jesus. I was ready.

I spent seventeen and one half years of my life as a pastor and being present with people through the last days before death.

I always shared the image of being taken up to God and God waiting with arms open wide!

I would talk about how we run into the strong, safe arms of God and we are lifted up as God swings us round and round with our feet flying out the back...just like we remember as a child.

I would often ask, "Can you imagine being a child again?"

It is a mystery being so full of life one second and dead the next. Dead is what we humans call it, but it is really a birthing into the arms of God. I was gifted with this heavenly image of birthing.

Someone once told me that being born into the next life is much like being born into this life.

I can't remember if I heard this in a talk on an Emmaus Walk, or in a class, or on a retreat, so whomever this belongs to, I cherish it and hope others will as well.

As a matter of fact, I remember Philip Newell speaking about this in the canyon in Oklahoma (one of my surreal places). My Celtic spirituality rises to the top again as I put these words to paper. I am sure it was Philip Newell who talked and wrote about this image, and I thank you Philip!

I became immersed in the image of birthing. Each human being is a soul that is placed in the womb by God in the very image of God. As each one of us grows in the womb, we become comfortable with our home that is warm and cozy and provides all the nourishment that we need.

All of our needs are taken care of even before they are needed. It is a welcoming place, and we are just as comfortable there as we can be.

And then the pushing begins and shoving and things seem to be very frightening. "What is happening?" And then after several hours of what seems like days and weeks, there is a final shove, and out we come! We are not cozy anymore! We are not warm!

We do not feel cuddled and safe or taken care of, and sometimes we feel pain on our bottom side and cry out! We do not like this, and it must be frightening! Everything we have ever known or experienced is taken away, just like that.

In a split second, life changes, and we are not happy about it because we do not understand what is happening. Fear takes over. We must be in crisis in the unknown. It is all a great mystery.

As time goes by, we are loved, we grow, we mature, and we become pretty amazing human beings with intelligence and grace. Life gets pretty comfortable. For the most part, we know what to expect...we carve out a life for ourselves, and we feel good about it.

Just about the time we are getting settled into our lives, another mystery happens. We begin to feel smaller, and we sometimes forget things, and it is not as easy to get around anymore; but, we love our life here on earth, and we fight as hard as possible to stay right where we are.

We do not like change, and want everything to just be like it has always been.

Our bodies and many times our minds begin to change, and life gets a little more difficult. **And then as we are fighting to keep what we know and what we are comfortable with,** another mystery happens.

We are pushed into another birthing canal, and we are frightened. We do not want to go, and yet that last final push has us sliding out the other side.

I cannot yet comment on what it might be like on the other side of this particular birthing canal, but I can only imagine that if this life was a pretty good one, the next will certainly be over the top!

And knowing humans as we do...if we can be born into this life and get comfortable and love it so much that we will fight not to leave it, then I have no words for the life with God face to face.

It is a great mystery, but the hope and joy and promise in the birthing image should turn our fear into hope and expectancy.

In a Split Second

This birthing image was obviously something that registered in the back of my mind when I thought I had been shot. I was ready to experience this mystery.

It was a mystery that I was covered in glass, yet felt no blood dripping. How could I be in this place at this time? Where was I anyway? I felt suspended in time.

Had my angels begun to accompany me into the birth canal to the next life? I was ready for them. I was looking for them. Let the birthing begin!

It is the image I have of crossing over to the "other side" of life on earth.

I did not understand why my angels were not present until I looked out the window (were my eyes closed as I drove this mile in shock?) and I remember thinking...I am not going yet...I am still here...on earth...it was a mystery.

The first recollection I have of the mystery of life and death was at age 12 when my maternal grandfather died.

He had been in the war and carried a wound that would not heal and finally killed him. I do not remember much about him except that he came to America to Ellis Island on a ship from Crete with all his possessions in a crate. He could not speak a word of English.

He met and married my grandmother who could not speak a word of Greek, and I do not know how they communicated but they did. What mystery there was in that relationship!

My grandfather was a chef, and I still remember the smells and the laughter when he was around, which wasn't often because he worked all the time. Laughter and food: that is how I remember Grandpa Nick.

When he died, all those around him were very vocal with the wailing and grieving, and I was allowed to go to the funeral. When my aunt took me up to the casket for a "viewing" and I saw him quite lifeless, I was stunned. Then my aunt made me touch him, and he was so cold and so not him that I fainted on the spot.

Needless to say, I did not attend another funeral until my father died. The mystery of it all had me frightened. It seemed upsetting to me that the God of life could also be the God of lifelessness as well.

The mystery continued to haunt me, but at age 17, I had an experience with God that was the beginning of my openness to life and death and the mystery of God. I am sharing an excerpt from my first book, *Little Bits and Bytes of Revelation: Messages from God*:

In a Split Second

A Bit of Knowing

Jeremiah 29:11 (New International Version)

11 *For I know the plans I have for you," declares the LORD, "plans to prosper you and not to harm you, plans to give you hope and a future.*

God Speaks

When I was 17 years old I was afraid of death and dying. I am not sure why I worried over it at that age, but I did.

As I remember, one night as I prayed before I went to sleep—I was praying to God to allow me to please have a child before I died. I have always loved children and having one of my own was my greatest desire.

Later that night I had a vision. I did not speak of it for ten years and only then did I speak of it very cautiously. As I remember it, God was in a sitting position; I was kneeling at God's feet. I remember looking up at God in awe; my arms crossed as my head leaned on my arms that were on God's lap.

We had quite a conversation, as I remember, but when I awoke I remembered one thing: I had assurance that I was not going to die any time soon and that God had a plan for my life.

I "know" that I was given detailed information but obviously it was important for me to remember only what God assured me of that night—that God had plans for my life.

I was so certain of this vision that I did not speak of it because it was sacred to me, and besides, many folks would think that I was crazy! It also frightened me a little.

God revealed to me that God does have plans for all God's children and we can have assurance...the details? We do not need to know the details....We need to believe, trust, and follow...not to take control...it is in God's hands.

My greatest desire for children was fulfilled: I have two daughters, one step-daughter, and twelve (at present) grandchildren and even now, I am living out God's plan for me. Besides being a grandmother many times over, I also am a child of God called to ministry...who'd have thought it when I was seventeen years old?

Blessed Assurance! I know God speaks.

In a Split Second

Know the hope…does God speak to you in dreams? Do not be afraid…God is gifting you hope in a way that God did even in Biblical times. Pray about what and how God speaks…know that you do not need all of the details…God takes care of those…just know that God has plans for you…and gives you hope…God speaks.

End excerpt. Little Bits and Bytes of Revelation: Messages from God is available on Amazon and Kindle. ISN 978-1449521868

This mystery has unfolded as the years have gone by and of course, I am now retired with 15 grandchildren and after 17 ½ years in ministry, I have had plenty of experience with death. The two times that are most meaningful to me and the joy in the birthing image follow:

Martha

Martha was a member in my third appointed church that I served in North Carolina. She was a small woman in her seventies. She came to church with her daughter. Martha was quite a character, and she loved me!

She was intentional about finding me after service and giving me a wonderful hug. Martha was full of life until she began to die.

Not long after my next appointment, which moved me away from that town, I got a call from Martha's daughter that said I needed to go and visit Martha in the hospital—that she was asking for me. That was all the info I had.

She called me to her hospital bed and told me that she was going to die soon. My heart struggled as she talked with me.

On my last and final visit, I sat on her bed cross-legged, and she smiled and told me that I had taught her how to trust God and so now she was not afraid to die because she knew that she was a Child of God and she could shout, "Yeah God!"

She asked me to preach her funeral, and as we talked about it, we laughed and cried, and I promised her I would shout for her—"Yeah God!"

The Holy Spirit had given her the confidence she needed through the preaching of God's word and my joy in shouting, "Yeah God!" God spoke to Martha through me to prepare her for her time of death. We read Psalm 30 about how God can turn a time of mourning into dancing!

A time of mourning turned to dancing as Martha and I

talked and laughed and prepared her funeral sermon. Her funeral was the most touching funeral I have experienced, and it was truly a time of dancing. A mystery indeed.

JoAnn

My most recent experience that molded mystery into joy and dancing was my friend JoAnn's illness and death. She was a member of my last appointed church and had been battling cancer long before I got there.

Even though she had battled cancer for some time, she was the most joyful person I have ever met! JoAnn was always positive, always joyful, always loving God.

She would come to the kneeling rail Sunday after Sunday and say, "I love you Lord, and I trust you no matter what!"

She was always helping others and donating her time and energy. When we realized that she was not going to overcome the last recurrence of cancer, it became difficult for the entire church to know what to say or do.

I asked JoAnn if we could walk this mysterious journey to the other side with her, and she agreed. Each week in worship we would talk about it and how she was doing and what we could all do to help.

One day I asked JoAnn if we could experience something on her bucket list with her. She thought about it and decided she wanted to go to Lake Junaluska in the North Carolina Mountains because she had never been to this place of beauty and nature and had heard how beautiful it was.

A couple of weeks later, there were six of us that packed up the church van and with the help of the congregation, we had funds for gas, lodging, and food as well as snacks.

We began our journey. We stopped often for JoAnn,

and we laughed and had the best time on JoAnn's bucket list trip.

When we arrived, the staff at the lodge where we stayed knew why we were there, and I can't express my appreciation in words for the kindness and caring they surrounded us with. We became like children again.

We boated on the lake, we had devotions in rocking chairs on the porch in the crisp morning air, we celebrated Holy Communion every day, and we walked a prayer labyrinth together. We laughed and cried, and we were surrounded by mystery.

We talked as we walked through the mountain woods, and JoAnn told us that she did not want a funeral. She did not want people being sad and crying because she was going to be dancing with Jesus. That was something to celebrate.

When we returned to her home and the church, she was exhausted, but so happy and content that we shared one of her bucket list wishes with her.

We turned the trip into a video to share with the whole church and put it to one of JoAnn's joyful songs:

Roberta Byram

"Where I Belong" by Building 429

Sometimes it feels like I'm watching from the outside
Sometimes it feels like I'm breathing but am I alive
I won't keep searching for answers that aren't here to
find

All I know is I'm not home yet
This is not where I belong
Take this world and give me Jesus
This is not where I belong

So when the walls come falling down on me
And when I'm lost in the current of a raging sea
I have this blessed assurance holding me.

All I know is I'm not home yet
This is not where I belong
Take this world and give me Jesus
This is not where I belong

When the earth shakes I wanna be found in You
When the lights fade I wanna be found in You

In a Split Second

All I know is I'm not home yet
This is not where I belong
Take this world and give me Jesus

JoAnn knew she was not home yet and there was joy in that for her right up to the very end! She did decide to let me throw a party in the guise of a funeral service.

We sang her favorite songs, we talked about her, and we threw the funeral book out the window!

Everyone sang, laughed, and remembered JoAnn in all her loving kindness and joy of the Lord and yes, on her grave stone she had engraved: *Dancing with Jesus!* A mystery not yet revealed to us.

Birthing into this life on earth and then back into the heavens with God, face to face. Crossing over through the birth canal. Being taken up. The mystery of it all.

Yes, my near-death experience was a mystery. I was not dead yet, my dancing partner was not swinging me round and round, and God was not finished with me yet here in this life on earth.

The mystery continued.

Roberta Byram

CHAPTER THREE: AWARENESS

I was not aware of the shattered glass all over me...yes, in my walking shoes, my clothes, and my hair. I was covered in blue-green pieces of glass. I was not aware of any pain or blood. Obviously, it came through the driver's side window (which was rolled up, thankfully).

I did became aware of my friend Mary. She turned my face toward her and said, "Thanks be to God, the side of your face is still there, and where is the blood?" She was terrified, but I was aware of the relief that washed over her face.

Of course it was my best friend Mary. She was right there beside me, and the calmness in her voice returned my sanity. I pulled over, and she put the car in park. The roles had changed in a split second. Me, I, Bert is the expert in crisis and well-trained. It is one of my strengths, and it has been part of my life for a very long time, but in this situation, I was not the one who showed strength in crisis...it was my friend Mary.

I looked at her and whispered, "I don't know what to do." We both said, "Call Tim" (my husband)...he always knows what to do. I recognized that I was in shock. Mary recognized that I was in shock.

I called my husband.

It happened in a split second. My husband was at his desk working and his wife calls and says, "I am ok but something just happened and I am covered in glass and a policeman is here and I can't talk now because I am in shock." And then I hung up.

Now, I can't imagine the fear in his mind. That is all that I told him. He tried to call back, but I had given my phone to the policeman, and he talked to Tim. I said to the policeman...I am in shock. He gently said, "Yes...I can see that."

I was aware that the policeman tried to keep the situation light to try to bring me out of it. He had been about four to five blocks behind us and saw what had happened and followed the trail of glass on the road.

In a Split Second

He smiled a large, bright, sunny smile and said, "Did you do all that littering on the road?"

Then he and Mary started bantering back and forth, and even in my state of shock, it was some comfort to me. This is the friend that I knew! Joking with a police officer!

My mind was stopped in time as they began to take care of the rental car and decide how to get us another one and what to do. I was aware of things at that point that seem now to be very strange.

I was aware that they were trying to get as much glass out of the driver's seat as possible. I was aware of them moving on to the back seat and Mary picking up several empty water bottles and telling the police officer that we were heavy drinkers and liked to party. (I remember thinking....why would she say that to a police officer?). His reply was simply, "I think you two are the party!"

At that time, I became aware of the landscape...for example, I noticed the mountains around us and the beauty they contained, the high grass that I was standing in, the bright and beautiful sunshine, remembering what a perfectly gorgeous day it was.

Roberta Byram

Why was I not tending to business like I always do?

I wonder if somewhere in the recesses of my mind I was noticing things that I am normally too busy to notice. So much of life happening around us and yet, we hurry through with our eyes closed.

I could feel the warm sun on my face and a gentle breeze and in my shock I think I smiled at that...but where was the blood?

The policeman asked for my driver's license and if I was wanted anywhere...trying to get a smile from me. "No, I am not wanted anywhere" was my quick answer to which Mary replied...."Yes she is! She is wanted in Raleigh...we all want her there!"

I wondered what she was talking about but gave him my license. He insisted that she drive the next couple of miles to where he was taking us, and I responded that she couldn't do that because we were in a rental car and I was the only driver (now, why was I being such a rule keeper at this moment when a policeman was giving me instructions)!

In a Split Second

He asked me if she had a license and if she was wanted anywhere, and I said she does and no she is not wanted in any state that I know of anyway.

Then the command in his voice got my attention, and I knew that Mary was going to drive.

All of this happened in a short amount of time. Simultaneously, I looked down where my feet were and I leaned down and just picked a four-leaf clover and put it in the policeman's pocket. Surely, he thought I was a crazy woman! Here I was in a crisis and in shock, and I pick a lucky clover and gift it to him???

Looking back, I wonder if this was a sign to all of us. A four leaf clover is good luck. I had good luck in that I was not dead on this day and I gave my luck to another.

Giving and receiving, being thankful and saying thank you in an unusual way. Being present and aware of what is before you in the midst of shock and crisis. Being aware of more going on here than one could imagine.

Awareness…in times of fear and crisis, our spiritual DNA will take over.

Having some Celtic spirituality in mine, I noticed the nature that God had created all around me to remind me that God is always present and that hope and promise are always there for all of us. It is our responsibility to be aware of it.

I totally put everything out of my mind with the exception of answering the questions being asked. I embraced the Creation and acknowledged the frailty of life. I was still here among the beautiful created order, and whether or not that should have been in my being at that moment, I praise God that I was aware of the His presence.

My poor husband. It was almost two hours before I could get back to him with some semblance of coherence. I do not think he was happy with me as I would not have been either. But we talked, and he could hear the calmness back in my voice. Together, we became aware of how one's life can change in a split second.

In a Split Second

I was not aware of the policeman a few blocks behind us on this drive through the town. I was not aware of the crisis at hand. I was not aware that the reason I was there in the first place did not seem so important anymore...even though it was very important.

I was not aware of the glass, the car, Mary for many seconds...I had not been aware of the mountains, sun, and beauty of the earth all around me.

How aware are we of what is happening around us?

I have had many experiences where I was not being aware, and I am embarrassed to admit that. How much of life have I missed because I was not paying attention? All wrapped up in work and getting things done and doing as much as humanly possible every day.

After several years of knowing that something was not right within me, I became aware through a long process that I have severe fibromyalgia and yes, it was diagnosed through blood tests...many, many tests.

But it did not start there....That was not the beginning....You see, I would not stop long enough to get the full picture—the big picture of what was happening to me.

So I began with a sleep study. I thought I was sleeping ok and was not aware at the time that this could be a problem.

I discovered that I had been waking up 36 times per minute every minute, and I became aware that I could have died in my sleep at any time due to lack of oxygen. Oh, did I mention that lack of oxygen to the brain also does strange things to your mind?

I would say things and do things and then not remember or spit something out that wasn't really me. I struggled everywhere but just thought I worked too much.

I also became aware that it is not just obese people who have sleep apnea (at the time of my study, I was not overweight at all) and was shown a whole wing of a building that focused on children with sleep apnea. I really was not aware of any of this, so into my career I was, you see.

Dying in my sleep was not an option so I did, of course, do what I was told to do (which I did not like...take a rest and use the equipment recommended). This is what I wrote in my journal after making this decision:

Rest

Where to begin

What should I work on

Stop mind—stop

I am not working now

No need to think and think and think

Only to enjoy and rest

To rest in God and heal

Heal me, Lord, heal me

Holy Spirit I beg you to help me forgive

Forgive all those I think have wronged me

The biggest one is myself

Help me pray for all of them

Yes including me

I want to forgive—desire it with all my heart.

I sit on the porch and listen to the birds.

I hear sounds I have not heard in a while.

Roberta Byram

I breathe in Creation and know

That I have missed it so.

My world has been one of work

Hurry and hurry and do as much as I can

Fill the days and nights with as much

As is humanly possible and yet

To save my life, You kept me alive

When I should have had a stroke

Or died in my sleep.

It was Your grace that saved me yet again.

And so I think that I will do this

I will dedicate this time to You

To respecting and caring for my body

My mind and my spirit—Your creation.

This will be our time, to reconnect, to heal

Physically, emotionally and spiritually

In a Split Second

Yes, this is what I'll do—I have missed You so.

Touch me, heal me, and call me back to You.

I love you more than life itself yet life itself

Got the best of me—that which belongs to You.

It happened ever so slowly and then years later

Caught in the web, I came to my senses

Because of my health, I came to my senses

And now I am on the road back home to You.

I was not aware that I could not do this in a week. As I write this now, I am aware of how sad I feel. Do I wish I could go back? Don't we all? It was a couple of years later when my body told me I was in trouble.

I paid attention and got the rest of the testing that I needed. When I was told that I must be on disability, I laughed and said, there is always another choice, so what is it?

I spent two years at the Duke Pain Clinic working toward how to live life with this terrible, painful condition.

Two years after that, I came up with a formula that allows me to live a somewhat normal life.

At least I was able to work (although most of my paycheck went to the formula...medication, deep-tissue massage therapy and reflexology, chiropractic, and acupuncture—all twice a month).

Do I still live with pain? Oh yes, I am quite aware of the pain that I live with every day, but I am so thankful that I am aware of this and know how to relieve it enough to function.

My colleagues were not aware of this condition and teased me about getting massages and said that I liked to spoil myself! They were not aware that they were very painful but necessary.

All this to say...it took something very painful physically and emotionally to open my eyes to a condition that I should have been aware of much earlier and dealt with at the time, but I did not take the time to be aware of what my body was telling me or see the signs from others that there was a problem.

In a Split Second

I was aware years later that stress made this condition much worse and that I could not work unless I gave my whole life to it, so I decided to retire early.

I am intentional about not being in a hurry or flying through my days.

I am so content to notice the day and all the changes that nature experiences in 24 hours—all of it is a gift to us. I smile a lot these days.

I am also thankful for two more things related to awareness.

Somewhere in my being, I took photos along the way of my life. And somehow, I managed to save many of them.

I am thankful to my sister Kathy for being assertive in her Fine Art America emails and texts that got me addicted to that website.

I became aware of the photos that I had taken during all the life that I had raced through and not taken time to enjoy, except for the time it takes to snap a camera.

I am now enjoying all those wonderful photos of all those wonderful places and beautiful lands, plants, trees, rocks, flowers….I am now aware of what I was not aware of at the time.

I am happy to share them with you as well on my website: http://bertsworks.com. I also share a blog on this website under the info tab. I hope you will take a few moments to enjoy and be aware of all that is around us.

There are 24 hours in our day...in just one day. So, the fortunate people sleep for eight hours of that day. That leaves 16 hours in just one day of our lives. How many split seconds is that? There are 57,600 seconds in just one of our days.

What have you noticed in just a portion of that one day? Are you aware of what is around you, or are you a bit like me...flying through each one at warp speed in order to fit as many things in one day as possible...things that are maybe not quite as important as we think they are in comparison to the big picture?

Becoming aware that our lives can change in a split second may find you thirsty for awareness of the things of life that bring hope and promise...take time to smell the roses, take some snapshots and save them, or pick the lucky clovers—it will make a difference in your life.

Chapter Four: Imagine

Imagine a second chance at life…what would you do? How would you react? Would your life be any different?

My life changed in a split second; I thought I was shot. It turns out that a rock from a weed whacker flew into my window just by my ear and bounced off the glass. Imagine that. A rock. I love rocks. That rock bounced off and I did not even get to hold it, look at it, or see it. Praise be to God!

I was not aware of the neighborhood activity as I drove through a community near where my mom was hospitalized. I was too busy talking to Mary and sharing the events leading to my mom's death, including the hospital stay. I had been so involved in describing everything as it had been with my mom, that I did not notice nor was I even aware that someone was outside on the lawn whacking the weeds near the street. If we had we been walking, this rock could have been as fatal as a gunshot.

The sound of it was like a shot, but things are not always as they seem.

I did not need to look for my angel escort, but it appeared to me as though I did. How often do we think things are a certain way and then we learn that they are not the way we thought they were at all? Interestingly enough, the event can change our lives whether it is so or not. Sometimes in a split second.

Am I aware of weed whackers now? You better believe it! As a matter of fact, I visited my daughter again and we were all playing cards at the table just like we always do and very involved as we are all very competitive...I heard, yes, you guessed it...a weed whacker. "Do you hear that?" I asked to everyone around the table. "Hear what?" they replied. "The weed whacker!" I exclaimed.

"Oh, that is the neighbor across the street," my daughter answered.

"Please will you go and move my car to the back...it is out front, and I do not want another broken window on a rental car....I can't do it myself!" I yelled. My daughter calmly got up, and the card game came to a halt. She moved the car for me and when she returned, we continued the game.

In a Split Second

I know she wondered at this strange reaction, but a weed whacker had changed my life in a split second, and I still responded with fear.

Can we even imagine a world without fear? What is it that you fear? Just imagine all of life that we miss because of fear, lack of awareness, lack of attention to mystery and really hearing the message offered to us.

Daniel

I met Daniel one Wednesday evening at Wednesday Night Church Dinner. I stopped and just stared at him. I went over and introduced myself. He said that his name was Daniel. I could not help staring at him. He looked just like my oldest grandson.

He was the same build and height, had on cowboy boots, and his mannerisms were the same. I later learned that he liked country western music and drove pickup trucks. He liked to work on cars and was a mechanic type. He was just like my grandson.

It took me a while to come to my senses. Immediately, I hugged him, and he asked me why I did that.

I told him he might as well be my grandson too, and from that moment on, Daniel and I were close. He began to come to church and got involved in the youth group. He also came to worship service.

Soon after that, he attended a Chrysalis Flight, a spiritual weekend for youth, and I was so excited that he had gone on such a weekend as this.

Later, he told me that it changed his life. Daniel struggled with communicating well. He was a slow reader and didn't speak well. It didn't matter to me, he was my adopted grandson, and I knew that he had great promise.

He graduated from high school and slacked off at church. It was summer and his family went to the beach a lot. He got a job and tried community college. I worried that he was slipping away from church and youth.

One day I got a phone call and then watched the news. Daniel had gotten in with the wrong crowd, and he made a terrible mistake. He was one to listen to authority and an authoritative adult told him to do something. It was a horrible nightmare.

In a Split Second

Daniel was in the county jail. My heart broke. I knew that Daniel could not have done what they said...according to the news...he must have been a mastermind and created quite a plot.

I was shocked...if not, I would have been laughing. That was not who Daniel was...no...but it was true that he was in the county jail, and I had to get to him.

It is amazing how quickly our lives can change. One of my young people at church was in jail, the one I considered like a grandson. I will tell you that the six months he was in the county jail were hell.

We prayed through a glass barrier between us, we cried through the glass, and we talked about how he could stay sane in there. It was really a very low point in my life and his. But God did not let us down. When it came time for him to go to prison, he was grounded.

He was adamant about one thing that he wanted to do when he got out. He was going to go to every youth group that would have him, and he was going to share from experience how one split second can change your life forever.

He would tell me how unreal it was when one minute he was sitting on the couch with his parents watching TV and after a phone call...and some orders that were given to him...one split second changed his life.

In that one split second when he turned and went out the door, his life became a five-year prison sentence resulting from a plea bargain.

Daniel was transformed in that county jail. We spent many visits talking about the visions he had, the experiences with God, and what it all meant to him.

He accepted Jesus as his path back to God and told me about prayer groups that he was starting in jail.

Once he told me that God had put his hand on him and given him the gift of speaking. Remember, Daniel's gift was not communicating well.

Until that split second when God's hand came upon him...and from that moment on when he spoke, I saw and heard the transformation, and it was quite a surprise to me.

In a Split Second

One day I was speaking to him and was at a loss for a word, and he gave it to me! I just couldn't believe it!

From then on, he was reading his Bible and books that I sent him. It was really a privilege to see him blossom…in, of all places…jail.

Oh, did I mention that he is an artist? He draws on any scrap of paper he can find.   I have included some of his drawings below and they are on my website (http://bertsworks.com).

In a Split Second

Daniel was then moved to a minimum-security prison. Prison is a sad place, even the minimum-security prisons.

I do not know how any young man who has made a mistake can recover from the experience.

It feels like you are always guilty of something going on in prison whether you are or not. Daniel has a large target on his back now. His head is down, he does not get into trouble and his reply to other inmates is this...I am focused on one thing—getting out of here, and I will not participate in anything that will keep that from happening.

Daniel spent his 21st and 22nd birthdays in prison. In one and one half years, he has been in five different locations.

When I say he has a target on his back...in one of the locations when he went out to work, a guard who spent too much time around Daniel and made a situation full of agitation, wrote him up for having too many clothes in his locker. Daniel spent 34 days in segregation and was cuffed and shackled and had marks on his wrists.

No, it does not matter if all of the inmates had the same number of socks and shirts...rules are rules, and Daniel is the one they made an example of—they sent him to medium security.

I praise God that 3 days after he got out of segregation, he was moved to another facility.

So, life in prison moves backward and not forward. In some of the facilities, not all, but in the ones I have visited...and then, on top of that, no one really cares about people who go to prison, do they?

And none of us want to hear about what really happens there...it might change our lives, and we would just rather not go there.

One split second changed Daniel's life forever. One split second changed my life forever. I pray that you will be aware of your life and all of life around you and not speed through it like I did.

Don't just ignore what is really happening to people, or you might experience that one split second and be totally unprepared.

In a Split Second

Daniel was aware of a song that we did a mime to at Youth Group before his situation. It is called *Give Me Your Eyes* by Brandan Heath. The youth made it real to us as they acted out what the words were telling us. These are the words:

"Give Me Your Eyes" by Brandon Heath

Looked down from a broken sky
Traced out by the city lights
My world from a mile high
Best seat in the house tonight
Touched down on the cold black top
Hold on for the sudden stop
Breathe in the familiar shock
Of confusion
And chaos

All those people goin' somewhere
Why have I never cared?

Give me Your eyes for just one second
Give me Your eyes so I can see

Everything that I keep missing
Give me Your love for humanity

Roberta Byram

Give me Your arms for the broken-hearted

The ones that are far beyond my reach
Give me Your heart for the ones forgotten
Give me Your eyes so I can see
Yeah
Yeah
Yeah
Yeah
Step out on a busy street
See a girl and our eyes meet
Does her best to smile at me
To hide what's underneath
There's a man just to her right
Black suit and a bright red tie
Too ashamed to tell his wife
He's out of work, he's buyin' time

All those people goin' somewhere
Why have I never cared?

Give me Your eyes for just one second
Give me Your eyes so I can see
Everything that I keep missing
Give me Your love for humanity

In a Split Second

Give me Your arms for the broken-hearted
The ones that are far beyond my reach

Give me Your heart for the ones forgotten
Give me Your eyes so I can see
Yeah
Yeah
Yeah
Yeah
I've been there a million times
A couple of million eyes
Just move and pass me by
I swear I never thought that I was wrong
Well I want a second glance
So give me a second chance
To see the way You've seen the people all along

Give me Your eyes for just one second
Give me Your eyes so I can see
Everything that I keep missing
Give me Your love for humanity
Give me Your arms for the broken-hearted
The ones that are far beyond my reach

Give me Your heart for the ones forgotten
Give me Your eyes so I can see

Roberta Byram

Give me Your Eyes (Give me Your eyes for just one
second)
Lord, give me Your eyes (Give me Your eyes so I can see)
Everything (Everything that I keep missing)
(Give me Your love for humanity)
Give me Your heart (Give me Your arms for the broken-
hearted)
For the broken hearted (The ones that are far beyond
my reach)
Give me Your heart (Give me Your heart for the ones
forgotten)
Lord, give me Your eyes (Give me Your eyes so I can see)

Just imagine how life would be if we were all aware of
the mystery of God and not only listened to God but
actually heard what he had to say and took it into our
very being.

In a Split Second

Roberta Byram

Chapter Five: Reconcile

My "almost" near death experience began my road to reconcile many things in my life. People are going to be who we are until we are willing to continue to stretch and grow and it may take an "almost" near death experience to get our attention.

I read several books after this experience that continued to change my life:

Rob Bell	What We Talk About When We Talk About God
	Jesus Wants to Save Christians
Don Miguel Ruiz	The Four Agreements
Marianne Williamson	Illuminati
Philip Newell	Every one of his books are excellent and brings us back to the heartbeat of God.

Books, spiritual retreats, experiences with other people, nature, and everything around us will help us to reconcile what we think we believe because we have been listening to what God wants us to believe through hearing.

When left to our human selves, we make a mess of things and we make up beliefs, rules, and such along the way to suit ourselves. It is quite a revelation when, in a split second, all the "stuff" we have added to our faith is suddenly not as important as seeing God in all of nature, in our actions, and in experiences with others.

For example, until a few years ago, there were possibilities that I would not even consider.

I hadn't even thought about possibilities because I was so set in my ways of thinking, beliefs, ideas, and I was right and if you did not agree, you were wrong.

I was good, and you were bad. My life was black and white. I had not even considered the possibility of gray in mystery!

In a Split Second

A very down to earth example of this was an activity for my retirement. I found myself writing this on my blog:

HELLO!
Right, wrong, good, or bad....I grew up thinking that everything in life was right, wrong, good, bad, black, white. It wasn't until my "well-seasoned" years, that I discovered possibilities!

I discovered colors, paths, gray, other people that were not like me and many different ways of doing the same things! You may laugh, but to me, it was such a marvelous discovery and I have said good bye to rigidity and hello to possibilities.

Just think about it. What possibilities are there in your life that you are missing because you aren't even acknowledging the possibility of possibilities?

Being a workaholic all my life, I never took time to paint or do anything that did not serve a purpose that day or rate being on my prioritized to do list.

However, I did always say that one day I was going to paint.

Roberta Byram

A couple of years ago I bought some canvas and paint and brushes from the local craft store. I was ready to do this! What to paint?

I just started...picked up the brush and started. I discovered that I love abstracts and painted a few.

A couple of months ago I discovered abstract on software for the photographs I have been taking!

I only have a distort option that gives me a couple of choices....but Hallelujah! I was having the time of my life with abstract paintings!

Once, I believed the only way to create an abstract was on canvas or paper. No, I never considered the possibility of digital. I wonder what other possibilities I am about to discover? What possibilities are there in your life? Have you even considered?

Roberta

In a Split Second

It may seem like a small thing this abstract painting, but what if you apply this to the very core of your life? Have you considered all your possibilities?

A few challenging questions to consider are these:

Do you remember a time when you were fully and completely giving attention…to anything?

If you thought you would be entering into the birth canal to the next life this very day, what would you do differently in your day?

What would you think about, what would be important to you, what would you be aware of, imagine, and what would you truly hear?

You see, the day we are born on earth, we begin our journey back to the birth canal and back to God and so we have a number of years to prepare and look forward to that destination. Do we enjoy the journey? Do we walk in the light of God that leads the way?

How easily are you swayed into the ideas of the world to take the journey in a way that humans have created?

Are you so busy trying to belong to something or to outdo or be like that you lose your attention span and your eyes become filmy and barely see the direction of the light?

The direction of the light is not nearly so important when you turn to so many other things...things that put you in the center of this life instead of God in the focus.

Whatever your spiritual heritage your ancestors claimed before you were born on this earth, take some time to study all the heritages and make your own decision on where your human ancestral spiritual DNA comes from.

Our divine spiritual DNA is from God, but what about our human ancestral spiritual DNA?

Jesus's human ancestral spiritual DNA was Jewish, and mine is Celtic. Imagine my surprise when I discovered that one of my great grandfathers was born in Edinburgh, Scotland! One of my grandfathers was born in Germany and the other in Crete; both near where the nomadic Celtics settled for a time. I did not consider the possibility that I could have Celtic ancestral spiritual DNA within me!

As a Christian, I study Jesus's human ancestral spiritual DNA because I want to know all about him, but that does not mean that I must have the same ancestral background!

So many possibilities before us in our life to be discovered and learned and enjoyed!

In a Split Second

What is important in your life? If you could take one thing with you into that birth canal leaving this earth, what would it be?

Sports, movies, video games, cell phone, TV, clothes, car, techy stuff, books, or something else? Maybe the stuff you inherited?

When you reconcile life and death and divine spirituality and you give your full attention to God, the day gifted to you and the gifts of creation all around you, a sense of being set free overwhelms you.

I really do wish I had not waited for an "almost" near-death experience to see the divine light clearly. For so many years, I was restricted by many things and did not realize it. I am thankful God got my total attention in order for film to be peeled off my eyes so the divine light could blind me.

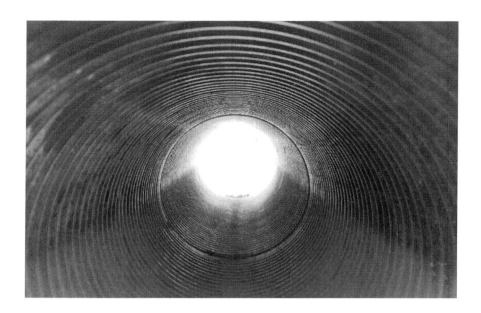

Oh, how I enjoy each and every day now. Oh, the beauty and creation that I notice *now*. I not only listen but I hear. I imagine the possibilities in life by being aware of the mystery of life on earth itself.

If you had a split second "almost" near-death experience today….what would you be reconciling in your life?

In a Split Second

"10,000 Reasons (Bless The Lord)" by Matt Redman

[Chorus]
Bless the Lord, O my soul
O my soul
Worship His holy name
Sing like never before
O my soul
I'll worship Your holy name

The sun comes up, it's a new day dawning
It's time to sing Your song again
Whatever may pass, and whatever lies before me
Let me be singing when the evening comes

[Chorus]
Bless the Lord, O my soul
O my soul
Worship His holy name

Sing like never before
O my soul
I'll worship Your holy name

You're rich in love, and You're slow to anger
Your name is great, and Your heart is kind

Roberta Byram

For all Your goodness I will keep on singing
Ten thousand reasons for my heart to find

[Chorus]
Bless the Lord, O my soul
O my soul
Worship His holy name
Sing like never before
O my soul
I'll worship Your holy name

And on that day when my strength is failing
The end draws near and my time has come
Still my soul will sing Your praise unending
Ten thousand years and then forevermore

[Chorus x2]
Bless the Lord, O my soul
O my soul
Worship His holy name
Sing like never before
O my soul
I'll worship Your holy name

Jesus, I'll worship Your holy name
Lord, I'll worship Your holy name

In a Split Second

Sing like never before
O my soul
I'll worship Your holy name
Jesus, I'll worship Your holy name
I'll worship Your holy name

Roberta Byram

We all take a journey here and there and everywhere; but the most significant journey we walk is our spiritual journey.

As you journey along, take time to see what God is placing before you, hear what God has to say to you, and be blessed that God chose you to be a channel of God's grace.

In a Split Second

Roberta Byram lives in Apex, North Carolina with her husband. She has fifteen grandchildren who are all ranges of age and personality, and she considers herself the most blessed grandmother. She spent over 20 years in the semiconductor industry (hardware) and traveled to Mexico and Europe. She then entered ministry and served 17 years as a United Methodist pastor in North Carolina.

She entered college at age 43 (North Carolina Wesleyan College) and earned a degree in Business Administration, and when she was 50, she entered graduate school (Duke Divinity School, Duke University) and earned a Master of Divinity at age 53. Roberta loves learning and is a life-long learner!

She was born and raised in Ohio about 40 miles southwest of Pittsburgh, Pennsylvania and has lived in south Georgia, Atlanta, Dallas, and now Raleigh, North Carolina. Roberta retired early to enjoy life, her grandchildren, writing, and photography.

She has a website: http://bertsworks.com where you can see her photographic work and read her blog. She knows these are her glory days! Every day is new and filled with wonder!

Proof

41513816R00061

Made in the USA
Charleston, SC
30 April 2015